The Pasta Lover Cookbook

How to Make Delicious Homemade Pasta – Mouthwatering Recipes

Discover the Delicious World of Pasta

By

Rola Oliver

License Notice

Table of Contents

Introduction

People have a general perception that meals consisting of pasta are bland. It is very clear that they have not yet sampled the appropriate pasta recipe!

You won't ever get tired of eating pasta if you make your way through *"The Pasta Lover's Cookbook,"* since it has such a wide variety of mouthwatering dishes that are cooked with an assortment of delectable ingredients in creative ways.

You'll learn how to make flavorful meals with well-cooked meat, healthy vegetables, and plenty of cheese, of course. Doesn't it just make your mouth water?

There is not a single recipe in this book that would be out of place at lunch, at the dinner table, or on a picnic. The nice part is that none of them needs much effort to put together.

Pasta and spaghetti are safe bets whenever you want to prepare something that is both straightforward and satisfying to eat.

wwwwwwwwwwwwwwwwwwwwwwwwwwww

1. Tuna fish pasta

Yield: 4 people

Preparation Time: 15 minutes

Ingredient List:

- 10 oz. of pasta
- 1 can of tuna fish
- 2 oz. of tomato sauce
- 1 shallot
- 2 tablespoons of olive oil
- Parmesan cheese
- A pinch of salt

wwwwwwwwwwwwwwwwwwwwwwwwwwwww

How to cook:

i. Bring the pasta to a boil in some lightly salted water and cook it according to the instructions on the package.

ii. Peel and chop the shallot, then fry it in olive oil.

iii. Add the tuna fish to the pan and fry it for a couple of minutes, then add the tomato sauce and bring the mixture to a boil.

iv. When the pasta is done, add it to the mix and cook it for just a couple more minutes.

v. Serve the tuna fish pasta with some grated Parmesan cheese on top.

2. Lemon flavored spaghetti

Yield: 4 people

Preparation Time: 20 minutes

Ingredient List:

- 10 oz. of spaghetti
- ½ lemon
- 1 stick of butter
- ½ cup of Parmesan cheese
- Chopped coriander
- Thyme
- A pinch of salt

wwwwwwwwwwwwwwwwwwwwwwwwwww

How to cook:

i. Bring the spaghetti to a boil in some lightly salted water and cook it according to the instructions on the package.

ii. Melt the stick of butter in a pan, add the squeezed juice from ½ a lemon, and the grated lemon zest as well.

iii. Add the pasta to the lemon sauce and cook it on a low flame for a couple more minutes, while continuously mixing.

iv. Add freshly chopped coriander, a pinch of thyme, and a pinch of salt (if necessary), and serve the lemon flavored spaghetti with some grated Parmesan cheese on top.

3. White pasta casserole

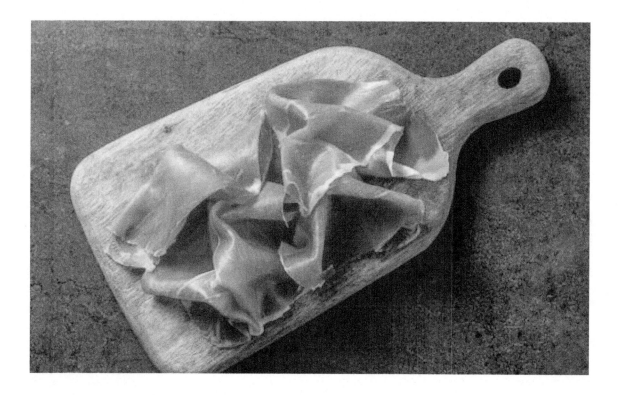

Yield: 4 people

Preparation Time: 40 minutes

Ingredient List:

- 10 oz. of pasta
- 7 oz. of prosciutto
- 1 clove of garlic
- 2 tablespoons of olive oil
- 10 oz. of Parmesan cheese
- 20 oz. of Bechamel sauce
- A pinch of salt and pepper

wwwwwwwwwwwwwwwwwwwwwwwwwwwwww

How to cook:

i. Bring the pasta to a boil in some lightly salted water and cook it according to the instructions on the package.

ii. Peel and chop the garlic, then fry it in oil.

iii. Add the diced prosciutto and fry until it becomes crisp.

iv. In a heat-resistant tray, mix the boiled pasta with the Bechamel sauce, prosciutto, and Parmesan cheese.

v. Bake the casserole at a temperature of 350°F, for about 10–15 minutes, until a crust forms on top.

vi. Once done, serve the white pasta casserole while it is still hot.

4. Zucchini bow-tie pasta

Yield: 4 people

Preparation Time: 20 minutes

Ingredient List:

- 10 oz. of bow-tie pasta
- 2 zucchinis
- 1 clove of garlic
- 1 tablespoon of extra virgin olive oil
- A pinch of salt and pepper

wwwwwwwwwwwwwwwwwwwwwwwwwww

How to cook:

i. Bring the bow-tie pasta to a boil in lightly salted water and cook it according to the instructions on the package.

ii. Wash and grate the zucchini.

iii. Fry the chopped garlic clove in olive oil.

iv. After a couple of minutes, add the grated zucchini.

v. Fry everything for about 5 minutes, then add the boiled pasta and mix everything together.

vi. Cook it for a few more minutes and, if necessary, add some cooking water from the pasta (add 1 ladle at a time).

vii. Add salt and pepper according to personal preference and serve the zucchini bow-tie pasta hot.

5. Cheesy fusilli

Yield: 4 people

Preparation Time: 15 minutes

Ingredient List:

- 10 oz. of fusilli
- 10 oz. of ricotta cheese
- 3 oz. of Parmesan cheese
- 3 oz. of sour cream
- Fresh thyme
- A pinch of salt and pepper

wwwwwwwwwwwwwwwwwwwwwwwwwwwww

How to cook:

i.   Bring the fusilli to a boil in some lightly salted water and cook it according to the instructions on the package.

ii.   Mix the ricotta cheese with the grated Parmesan and some fresh thyme. Add salt and pepper to taste.

iii.   Mix the cooked pasta with the cheese and serve the cheesy fusilli cold.

6. Cold vegetable pasta

Yield: 4 people

Preparation Time: 40 minutes

Ingredient List:

- 10 oz. of pasta
- 1 carrot
- 10–12 cherry tomatoes
- 1 zucchini
- 3 oz. of cheddar cheese
- 3 tablespoons of extra virgin olive oil
- 1 cup of mayonnaise (optional)
- Fresh basil
- A pinch of salt and pepper

wwwwwwwwwwwwwwwwwwwwwwwwwwwww

How to cook:

i. Bring the pasta to a boil in some lightly salted water and then cook it according to the instructions on the package. Once the pasta is ready, add some oil and set it aside to cool down.

ii. Wash and dice the carrots and zucchini, then (separately) bring them to a boil in some lightly salted water and cook them until they become tender. Let the vegetables cool after cooking.

iii. Wash and cut the cherry tomatoes in halves, then dice (or grate) the cheese.

iv. In a large bowl, mix everything together: the pasta, zucchini, carrots, cherry tomatoes and cheese.

v. Add fresh chopped basil, salt, and pepper to taste and (optionally) add and mix everything with a few tablespoons of mayonnaise.

vi. Once done, you have yourself some cold vegetable pasta.

7. Smoked salmon & pesto spaghetti

Yield: 4 people

Preparation Time: 30 minutes

Ingredient List:

- 10 oz. of spaghetti
- 6 oz. of smoked salmon
- 5–6 tablespoons of pesto sauce
- 3 oz. of sour cream
- 2 tablespoons of olive oil
- Parmesan cheese
- A pinch of salt

wwwwwwwwwwwwwwwwwwwwwwwwwwwwww

How to cook:

i. Bring the spaghetti to a boil in some lightly salted water and cook it according to the instructions on the package.

ii. Meanwhile, chop the smoked salmon and fry it in 2 tablespoons of olive oil.

iii. After a couple of minutes, add the sour cream, the pesto, and, when it has cooked, drain the spaghetti.

iv. Cook everything for a couple more minutes and serve the smoked salmon and pesto spaghetti with some grated Parmesan cheese on top.

8. Creamy eggplant spaghetti

Yield: 4 people

Preparation Time: 30 minutes

Ingredient List:

- 10 oz. of spaghetti
- 5 oz. of Ricotta cheese
- 1 eggplant
- 3 tablespoons of extra virgin olive oil
- Vegetable oil (for frying)
- Fresh basil
- A pinch of salt and pepper

wwwwwwwwwwwwwwwwwwwwwwwwwwww

How to cook:

i. Bring the spaghetti to a boil in some lightly salted water and cook it according to the instructions on the package.

ii. In a blender, add the cheese, extra virgin olive oil, fresh basil, salt, and pepper to taste and blend until the mixture is smooth in consistency.

iii. Wash and cut the eggplant into thin strips and fry them in vegetable oil, until they turn brown in color.

iv. In a large pan, heat up the cream cheese sauce and add the spaghetti to it.

v. Cook it for a couple of minutes, until the spaghetti and cream together blend well.

vi. Add the fried eggplant strips and serve the creamy eggplant spaghetti hot.

9. Savory bell pepper pasta

Yield: 4 people

Preparation Time: 45 minutes

Ingredient List:

- 10 oz. of pasta
- 1 red bell pepper, 1 yellow bell pepper, 1 green bell pepper
- 1 shallot
- 5 oz. of tomato sauce
- 3 tablespoons of olive oil
- Parmesan cheese
- Fresh basil
- A pinch of salt

wwwwwwwwwwwwwwwwwwwwwwwwwwww

How to cook:

i. Bring the pasta to a boil in some lightly salted water and cook it according to the instructions on the package.

ii. Peel and chop the shallot, then fry it in olive oil.

iii. Add the bell peppers, diced or cut in thin stripes, and fry them for a few minutes.

iv. Add the tomato sauce, a couple of fresh basil leaves, and enough water to cover the bell peppers, then continue cooking on a low flame.

v. Add the cooked pasta to the bell peppers, mix well, and cook for a couple more minutes.

vi. Serve the savory bell pepper pasta with some grated Parmesan on top.

10. Shrimp tail & zucchini pasta

Yield: 4 people

Preparation Time: 40 minutes

Ingredient List:

- 10 oz. of pasta
- 5 oz. of shrimp tail
- 1 zucchini
- 3 oz. of sour cream
- 1 shallot
- 3 tablespoons of extra virgin olive oil
- A pinch of salt and pepper

wwwwwwwwwwwwwwwwwwwwwwwwwwwwww

How to cook:

i.   Bring the pasta to a boil in some lightly salted water and cook it according to the instructions on the package.

ii. Peel and chop the shallot, wash and cut the zucchini into thin strips and peel the shrimp tails.

iii. Fry the shallot in olive oil, then add the zucchini and the shrimp, add salt and pepper to taste, and cook until the shrimp are done.

iv. Add the sour cream, mix well, and cook it for a few more minutes.

v.   Mix the pasta with the shrimp and zucchini and serve the shrimp tail and zucchini pasta hot.

11. Pasta with fried potatoes

Yield: 4 people

Preparation Time: 45 minutes

Ingredient List:

- 7 oz. of pasta
- 20 oz. of potatoes
- 1 shallot
- 3 tablespoons of olive oil
- Fresh rosemary and thyme
- A pinch of salt and pepper

wwwwwwwwwwwwwwwwwwwwwwwwwwww

How to cook:

i. Peel the potatoes and dice them.

ii. Fry the chopped shallot in olive oil, then add some fresh chopped rosemary and thyme.

iii. Add the potatoes and fry them until they're done (stir constantly so they won't burn).

iv. Bring the pasta to a boil in some lightly salted water and cook it according to the instructions on the package.

v. When done, drain the pasta and add it to the potatoes.

vi. Mix well, add salt and pepper to taste, and serve the pasta with warm fried potatoes.

12. Spaghetti "cacio e pepe"

Yield: 4 people

Preparation Time: 20 minutes

Ingredient List:

- 10 oz. of spaghetti
- 7 oz. of Pecorino cheese
- A pinch of salt
- A pinch of pepper

wwwwwwwwwwwwwwwwwwwwwwwwwwwwww

How to cook:

i. Bring the spaghetti to a boil in some lightly salted water and boil it according to the instructions on the package.

ii. Add pepper according to personal preference directly in the spaghetti cooking water and cook until the spaghetti is done.

iii. Alternatively (if you can handle the spicy flavor), bring a couple of ladles of the cooking water to a boil and add pepper according to personal liking. When the spaghetti is almost done, transfer them to the pepper-flavored water and cook for a couple more minutes.

iv. In a bowl, grate the Pecorino cheese and add 1 ladle of the cooking water to it. Mix well until it becomes creamy.

v. Mix the creamy cheese with the spaghetti and cook for a couple more minutes.

vi. Serve the spaghetti "cacio e pepe" with some extra grated Pecorino cheese on top.

13. Orange flavored fettuccine

Yield: 4 people

Preparation Time: 35 minutes

Ingredient List:

- 10 oz. of fettuccine
- 1 orange
- 1 stick of butter
- 2 oz. of Parmesan cheese
- Fresh chopped chives
- A pinch of salt and pepper

wwwwwwwwwwwwwwwwwwwwwwwwwwww

How to cook:

i. Peel the zest from the orange and cut it into thin stripes.

ii. Bring the fettuccine to a boil in some lightly salted water. Add most of the orange zest to the cooking water and cook it according to the instructions on the package.

iii. Finely chop the remaining orange zest, and fry it in a pan with some butter.

iv. When the fettuccine is almost cooked, add them to the pan and cook them in the orange-flavored butter for a few more minutes.

v. Add fresh chopped chives and grated Parmesan cheese and serve the orange flavored fettuccine.

14. Fettuccine with mushrooms

Yield: 4 people

Preparation Time: 50 minutes

Ingredient List:

- 10 oz. of fettuccine
- 10 oz. of fresh Champignon mushrooms
- 1 stick of butter
- 2 tablespoons of extra virgin olive oil
- 1 clove of garlic
- Fresh chopped parsley
- A pinch of salt

wwwwwwwwwwwwwwwwwwwwwwwwwwwww

How to cook:

i. Bring the fettuccine to a boil in some lightly salted water and cook it according to the instructions on the package.

ii. Wash and slice the mushrooms, then fry them with the chopped garlic in olive oil and butter until they're done. Add salt according to personal liking.

iii. When the mushrooms are cooked, add the fettuccine and mix well, then cook it for a few more minutes. If the pasta is too dry, add some cooking water to it (1 ladle at a time).

iv. Add fresh chopped parsley and serve the fettuccine with mushrooms hot.

15. Raisins spaghetti pudding

Yield: 4 people

Preparation Time: 1 hour

Ingredient List:

- 15 oz. of spaghetti
- 5 eggs
- 5 oz. of milk
- ½ cup of sugar
- ½ cup of raisins
- 1 stick of butter
- A pinch of salt

wwwwwwwwwwwwwwwwwwwwwwwwwwww

How to cook:

i. Bring the spaghetti to a boil in some lightly salted water and cook it according to the instructions on the package.

ii. Beat the eggs with the milk, and the sugar and add a pinch of salt.

iii. Add the cooked spaghetti and raisins to the mix and stir well.

iv. Grease a heat-resistant tray with some butter and pour in the spaghetti pudding.

v. Bake it at a temperature of 350°F, until it turns brown in color.

vi. Once done, you have yourself raisins spaghetti pudding.

16. Pasta cooked in ricotta and walnut sauce

Yield: 4 people

Preparation Time: 20 minutes

Ingredient List:

- 10 oz. of pasta
- 13 oz. of ricotta cheese
- ½ cup of toasted walnuts
- 1 tablespoon of extra virgin olive oil
- A pinch of salt and pepper

wwwwwwwwwwwwwwwwwwwwwwwwwwwwww

How to cook:

i. Bring the pasta to a boil in some lightly salted water and cook it according to the instructions on the package.

ii. Meanwhile, heat up the olive oil and add the ricotta cheese to the pan. Add a couple of ladles of cooking water from the pasta, add the toasted walnuts as well, and mix everything together.

iii. Add salt and pepper to taste and bring the sauce to a boil.

iv. When the pasta is almost done, add it to the cheese sauce and cook it for a couple more minutes.

v. Once done, you have yourself pasta cooked in ricotta and walnut sauce.

17. Baked macaroni and egg casserole

Yield: 4 people

Preparation Time: 40 minutes

Ingredient List:

- 10 oz. of pasta
- 5 oz. of cottage cheese
- 5 oz. of ricotta cheese
- 5 eggs + 1 yolk
- 10 tablespoons of sour cream
- 1 tablespoon of butter
- A pinch of salt
- Sugar (optional)

wwwwwwwwwwwwwwwwwwwwwwwwwwwww

How to cook:

i. Bring the pasta to a boil in some lightly salted water and cook it according to the instructions on the package.

ii. Beat the eggs and mix in the cheeses with 5 tablespoons of sour cream. Add salt according to personal liking.

iii. When the pasta is cooked, mix it with the eggs and pour it into a heat-resistant tray, previously coated with butter.

iv. Add a layer of sour cream mixed with 1 yolk on top and bake it at a temperature of 350°F, for a period of 15–20 minutes.

v. (optional) Serve the baked macaroni and egg casserole with some sugar.

18. Meatball pasta casserole

Yield: 4 people

Preparation Time: 2 hours

Ingredient List:

- 10 oz. of pasta
- 10 oz. of cheddar cheese
- 30 oz. of Bechamel sauce
- A pinch of salt and pepper

For the meatballs:

- 10 oz. of ground meat
- 2–3 slices of bread
- 2 eggs
- 1 clove of garlic
- 3–4 tablespoons of grated Parmesan cheese
- Fresh chopped parsley

For the sauce:

- 1 onion
- 30 oz. of tomato sauce
- 1 clove of garlic
- 3 tablespoons of extra virgin olive oil
- Fresh basil

How to cook:

Meatballs:

i. Mix the ground meat with the 2 eggs, the grated parmesan cheese, the slices of bread, and fresh chopped parsley. Add salt and pepper according to personal liking.

ii. Mix well then shape walnut-sized meatballs with your hands and set them aside while you prepare the rest.

Sauce:

i. Fry the chopped onion and garlic in olive oil.

ii. Add the tomato sauce and some fresh chopped basil, and bring the mixture to a boil.

Prepare the pasta casserole:

i. Add the meatballs to the sauce and bring it to a boil again.

ii. Add salt and pepper to taste and cook the meatballs for a period of 15–20 minutes, on a low flame.

iii. Bring the pasta to a boil in some lightly salted water and cook it according to the instructions on the package.

iv. When cooked, mix the pasta with the meatballs and sauce.

v. In a heat-resistant tray, add a layer of bechamel sauce, then a layer of pasta with meatballs, then another layer of bechamel sauce on top.

vi. Add a layer of grated cheddar cheese and bake it at a temperature of 350°F, for about 15–20 minutes, until a crust forms on top.

19. Spaghetti omelet

Yield: 4 people

Preparation Time: 30 minutes

Ingredient List:

- 10 oz. of spaghetti
- 5 eggs
- 5 oz. of grated cheddar cheese
- 1 clove of garlic
- 3 tablespoons of olive oil
- 3 oz. of milk
- A pinch of salt and pepper

wwwwwwwwwwwwwwwwwwwwwwwwwwwwww

How to cook:

i. Bring the spaghetti to a boil in some lightly salted water and cook it according to the instructions on the package.

ii. Beat the eggs with a pinch of salt and pepper and add the grated cheese and milk.

iii. Fry the chopped garlic in olive oil, then add the cooked spaghetti and cook it for a few minutes.

iv. Add the beaten eggs on top of the spaghetti, cover the pan, and cook it on a low flame for a few minutes (5–10), without stirring.

v. With the help of the lid, flip the omelet to the other side and cook until it is done.

vi. Once done, you have yourself a spaghetti omelet.

20. Spaghetti with meatballs

Yield: 4 people

Preparation Time: 2 hours

Ingredient List:

- 10 oz. of spaghetti
- 1 shallot
- 30 oz. of tomato sauce
- 1 clove of garlic
- 3 tablespoons of extra virgin olive oil
- Fresh basil
- A pinch of salt and pepper

For the meatballs:

- 10 oz. of ground meat
- 2–3 slices of bread
- 2 eggs
- 1 clove of garlic
- 3–4 tablespoons of grated Parmesan cheese
- Fresh chopped parsley

How to cook:

Meatballs:

    i.   Mix the ground meat with the eggs, grated cheese, slices of bread, and chopped parsley. Add salt and pepper according to personal liking.

    ii.   Mix the ingredients together well then shape the mixture into walnut-sized meatballs using your hands and set them aside while you prepare the rest.

Tomato sauce:

    i.   Fry the chopped shallot and garlic in olive oil.

    ii.   Add the tomato sauce and some fresh chopped basil and bring the mixture to a boil.

    iii.   Add the meatballs to the sauce and bring it to a boil

    iv.   Cook until the meatballs are done (for about 30 minutes).

Prepare the spaghetti with meatballs:

    i.   Bring the spaghetti to a boil in some lightly salted water and cook it according to the instructions on the package.

    ii.   Mix the cooked pasta with the meatball sauce and serve it hot.

21. Fettuccine Alfredo

Yield: 4 people

Preparation Time: 35 minutes

Ingredient List:

- 10 oz. of fettuccine
- 3 oz. of butter
- 3 oz. of Parmesan cheese
- A pinch of salt and pepper

wwwwwwwwwwwwwwwwwwwwwwwwwwwwwww

How to cook:

i.   Bring the fettuccine to a boil in some lightly salted water and cook it according to the instructions on the package.

ii. Meanwhile, melt the butter in a pan, then add a ladle of the pasta's cooking water.

iii. When the fettuccine is almost cooked, add it to the butter and cook it for a few more minutes, while swirling constantly. Add more cooking water if necessary.

iv. Add the grated cheese as soon as you take the pasta off the flame. Mix until the cheese melts, add salt and pepper ,according to personal liking and serve the fettuccine alfredo hot.

22. Crunchy walnut pasta

Yield: 4 people

Preparation Time: 30 minutes

Ingredient List:

- 10 oz. of pasta
- 5 oz. of walnuts
- 1 tablespoon of cinnamon
- 5 tablespoons of sugar
- 5 tablespoons of bread crumbs
- Sour cream
- A pinch of salt

wwwwwwwwwwwwwwwwwwwwwwwwwwwww

How to cook:

i. Bring the pasta to a boil in some lightly salted water and cook it according to the instructions on the package.

ii. Meanwhile, finely chop the nuts (using a knife or food processor) and toast them directly in the pan, tossing them around constantly to avoid them burning.

iii. Separately, toast the breadcrumbs directly in a large pan, while stirring constantly.

iv. When the bread crumbs start to brown, add the sugar and toasted walnuts, then add the cooked pasta and mix everything together well.

v. Serve the crunchy walnut pasta hot with sour cream on top. Add more sugar if necessary.

23. Four cheese pasta

Yield: 4 people

Preparation Time: 30 minutes

Ingredient List:

- 10 oz. of pasta
- 3 oz. of blue cheese
- 3 oz. of Parmesan cheese
- 3 oz. of cheddar cheese
- 3 oz. of mozzarella cheese
- 5 oz. of milk
- A pinch of salt and pepper

wwwwwwwwwwwwwwwwwwwwwwwwwwwwwww

How to cook:

i. Bring the pasta to a boil in some lightly salted water and cook it according to the instructions on the package.

ii. Meanwhile, dice the mozzarella, blue cheese, and cheddar, and grate the Parmesan.

iii. In a pan, heat up the milk and add the cheeses. Stir well until they melt.

iv. When almost cooked, add the pasta to the cheese sauce and mix well.

v. Cook it for another few minutes, add salt and pepper according to personal liking and serve the four cheese pasta hot.

24. Baked ragu pasta

Yield: 6 people

Preparation Time: 1 hour + 30 minutes

Ingredient List:

- 10 oz. of pasta
- 15 oz. of ground meat
- 4 oz. of tomato sauce
- 7 oz. of mozzarella cheese
- 2 tablespoons of olive oil
- 1 shallot
- A pinch of salt and pepper
- Breadcrumbs

wwwwwwwwwwwwwwwwwwwwwwwwwwwww

How to cook:

i. Bring the pasta to a boil in some lightly salted water and cook it according to the instructions on the package.

ii. Fry the chopped shallot in olive oil, then add the ground meat and cook until it changes color. Add salt and pepper according to personal liking.

iii. Add the tomato sauce and water (enough to cover the meat) and bring the mixture to a boil.

iv. When the pasta is almost cooked, add it to the ragu, mix well, and transfer everything to a heat-resistant tray.

v. Add the diced mozzarella cheese and a layer of breadcrumbs on top.

vi. Bake it at a temperature of 350°F, for a period of 35–40 minutes.

vii. Once done, you have yourself baked ragu pasta.

25. Stuffed pasta shells

Yield: 4 people

Preparation Time: 2 hours

Ingredient List:

- 10 oz. of pasta shells
- 2 eggplants
- 2 zucchinis
- 7 oz. of mozzarella cheese
- ½ cup of grated Parmesan cheese
- 15 oz. of tomato sauce
- ½ cup of diced olives
- 1 clove of garlic
- Vegetable oil
- 1 cup of all-purpose flour
- A pinch of salt and pepper

wwwwwwwwwwwwwwwwwwwwwwwwwwwwww

How to cook:

i. Wash and dice the eggplants and zucchini, salt them then set them aside for half an hour.

ii. Meanwhile, chop the garlic clove and fry it in oil. Add the diced olives and, after a couple of minutes, add the tomato sauce and bring it to a boil

iii. Cook it for at least half an hour, then add salt and pepper according to personal preference.

iv. After draining the excess liquid from the vegetables, coat them with flour and fry them in vegetable oil until they are brown and crispy.

v. Mix the crisp vegetables with the tomato sauce.

vi. Bring the pasta shells to a boil in some lightly salted water and cook it according to the instructions on the package.

vii. When the pasta shells are done, carefully stuff each one with the sauce and gently place each shell in a heat-resistant tray greased with some butter or oil.

viii. Add the remaining sauce with vegetables on top, as well as any remaining broken pieces of pasta shells.

ix. Add the diced mozzarella and a generous layer of grated Parmesan.

x. Bake it at a temperature of 350°F, for about 30 minutes, until a crust forms on top.

xi. Once done, you have yourself baked stuffed pasta shells.

26. Baked pasta in tomato sauce

Yield: 6 people

Preparation Time: 1 hour

Ingredient List:

- 10 oz. of pasta
- 7 oz. of salami slices
- 7 oz. of diced prosciutto
- 5 oz. of Parmesan cheese
- 5 oz. of mozzarella cheese
- 5 oz. of cheddar cheese
- 30 oz. of tomato sauce
- 1 shallot
- 1 clove of garlic
- Fresh basil & thyme
- Extra virgin olive oil
- A pinch of salt

wwwwwwwwwwwwwwwwwwwwwwwwwwwww

How to cook:

   i.   Fry the chopped shallot and garlic in olive oil, then add the tomato sauce and fresh basil and bring it to a boil. Add salt and pepper to taste.

   ii.   Bring the pasta to a boil in some lightly salted water and cook it according to the instructions on the package.

   iii. When the pasta is almost cooked, drain it and add it to the tomato sauce.

   iv. Add the diced prosciutto and salami, as well as the diced cheddar and mozzarella.

   v.   In a heat-resistant tray, add a layer of pasta, and continue with a layer of grated Parmesan and another layer of pasta.

   vi. Add the rest of the grated Parmesan on top and bake at a temperature of 350°F, for a period of 15–20 minutes.

   vii. Once done, you have yourself baked pasta in tomato sauce.

27. Spaghetti with garlicky pesto

Yield: 4 people

Preparation Time: 20 minutes

Ingredient List:

- 10 oz. of spaghetti
- 4 oz. of pesto sauce
- 1 clove of garlic
- 3 oz. of extra virgin olive oil
- Parmesan cheese
- A pinch of salt and pepper

wwwwwwwwwwwwwwwwwwwwwwwwwwww

How to cook:

i. Bring the spaghetti to a boil in some lightly salted water and cook it according to the instructions on the package.

ii. Fry the chopped garlic clove in olive oil, then add the pesto and 1 ladle of cooking water from the pasta.

iii. When the spaghetti is done, drain and mix it with the garlicky pesto sauce.

iv. Serve the spaghetti with garlicky pesto sauce hot with some grated Parmesan cheese on top.

28. Spicy sausage pasta

Yield: 4 people

Preparation Time: 30 minutes

Ingredient List:

- 10 oz. of pasta
- 1 zucchini
- 10 oz. of chorizo sausage
- 1 shallot
- 1 clove of garlic
- Swiss cheese
- 3 tablespoons olive oil
- A pinch of salt and pepper

wwwwwwwwwwwwwwwwwwwwwwwwwwwww

How to cook:

i. Bring the pasta to a boil in some lightly salted water and cook it according to the instructions on the package.

ii. Meanwhile, cut the zucchini and sausage into rounds.

iii. Fry the chopped shallot and chopped garlic clove in olive oil for a couple of minutes.

iv. Add the sausage and zucchini as well and cook them for a few minutes until they're done.

v. When the pasta is done, add it to the spicy sausage and mix them together well.

vi. Serve the spicy sausage pasta hot, with some grated cheese on top.

29. Crisp mac & cheese

Yield: 6 people

Preparation Time: 1 hour

Ingredient List:

- 20 oz. of macaroni
- 1 stick of butter
- 7 oz. of cheddar cheese
- 7 oz. of Swiss cheese
- 3 oz. of Parmesan cheese
- 30 oz. of Bechamel sauce
- A pinch of salt and pepper
- Breadcrumbs

wwwwwwwwwwwwwwwwwwwwwwwwwwww

How to cook:

i. Bring the macaroni to a boil in some lightly salted water and cook it according to the instructions on the package.

ii. Meanwhile, chop or grate the cheeses separately.

iii. Prepare the cheese cream: heat up the Bechamel sauce and add the Swiss and cheddar cheese to it. Mix well until they have melted.

iv. Grease a heat-resistant tray with butter then coat it with breadcrumbs.

v. Add the macaroni and cheese bechamel sauce to the tray and cover it with a layer of grated Parmesan cheese and breadcrumbs (this will help form a crunchy crust).

vi. Bake it at a temperature of 350°F, for a period of 25–30 minutes.

vii. Once done, you have yourself crispy mac and cheese.

30. Vegetable ragu pasta

Yield: 4 people

Preparation Time: 40 minutes

Ingredient List:

- 10 oz. of pasta
- 1 zucchini
- 10 oz. of Champignon mushrooms
- 3 oz. of cherry tomatoes
- 1 shallot
- Fresh chopped parsley
- 3 tablespoons of olive oil
- Parmesan cheese
- A pinch of salt and pepper

wwwwwwwwwwwwwwwwwwwwwwwwwwwwww

How to cook:

i.   Wash and dice the mushrooms, zucchini, and cherry tomatoes, and finely chop the shallot.

ii. In a large pan, fry the shallot in olive oil, then add the mushrooms and, when they become soft (after about 10 minutes), add the zucchini and cherry tomatoes.

iii. Add salt and pepper to taste and cook until the vegetables are tender.

iv. Meanwhile, bring the pasta to a boil in some lightly salted water and cook it according to the instructions on the package.

v.   When the pasta is ready, add it to the vegetable ragu, along with some fresh chopped parsley, and mix them together well.

vi. Serve the vegetable ragu pasta hot with some grated Parmesan cheese.

Author's Afterthoughts

thank you

FOR YOUR ORDER

Practice makes perfect in the same way that expressing gratitude paves the way to success because it allows you to become surrounded by people who know how much you value them in your journey. I've been blessed to have a loving family, amazing friends, and beautiful readers like you who support me and push me to constantly improve by trying out my recipes!

I'm so grateful that I'd like to give back to you and all of my readers by asking what kind of content you'd like to see more of. Is it a book on a particular cuisine or cooking style? Would you like me to work on more weeknight recipes? I'm excited to know what your thoughts are so I can start brainstorming on my next cookbook! I read all of my replies, reviews, and suggestions, so don't hesitate to leave me a comment because I WILL get to it and put it to good use in my writing and cooking.

Thanks a bunch!

Rola Oliver

About the Author

Cooking never really interested Rola until her family moved to Connecticut and the kids at her school began making fun of her because of her southern accent. From middle school all the way up to high school, Rola spent her afternoons at home. While life passed her by, her Nana was always in kitchen up to something delicious. Sometimes it would smell like onion, others of pie. Although Rola rarely left the sofa, her mind would wander to so many places with the smell of Nana's cooking. And when she ate, the flavors always surprised her!

Eventually, Nana was able to get Rola into the kitchen without saying a single word. The sounds of the kitchen knives and pans were a comforting feeling because they reminded her of Nana, her favorite person in the world.

At first, Rola spent up to 20 minutes chopping an onion… but fast forward twenty five years and Rola is now a celebrated southern cook in Connecticut! Nana isn't usually cooking anymore, but every now and then she still likes to pop in and watch her granddaughter at work. Together, they own a growing southern food joint, working hard to preserve traditions and authentic southern flavors.

Printed in Great Britain
by Amazon

21617036R00045